HOW TO HUSTLE

24/7

RATHER THAN

WORK 9 TO 5

THE HUSTLERS PAMPHLET

AUTHOR BIOGRAPHY

Brian Ernest Hayward is a passionate Author and Inspirational Speaker, internationally known for his unwavering dedication to creating positive change through the power of words. From religious and success books, to adult coloring books and artist BUSINESS, HOW-TO BOOKS, his writings touch on over 400 different subjects. Today, all of Brian's publications are sold worldwide across multiple formats (Paperback, Kindle, and Large Print) and are translated into 21 different languages. He has also participated in over 100 speaking engagements spanning over 38 states.

Table Of Contents

"How to Hustle Twenty 47,
Rather Than Slave 9 to 5:
The Hustlers Pamphlet"

Introduction

Welcome, dear reader, to "How to Hustle Twenty 47, Rather Than Slave 9 to 5: The Hustlers Pamphlet." This is not just a book; it is a manual for transforming your life. Whether you are stuck in  the monotonous cycle of a 9 to 5 job or simply looking for ways to maximize your potential, you have come to the right place. Over the following chapters, you will discover the secrets to breaking free from the traditional work routine and embracing a dynamic, goal-oriented lifestyle that leverages every moment to its fullest.

The idea for this book was born from a simple observation: the world is changing rapidly, and the traditional 9-to-5 job model no longer fits the aspirations of many individuals. People crave flexibility, creativity, and the ability to pursue their passions without being confined to a rigid schedule. This book took three months to write, with each month dedicated to meticulously researching, compiling, and refining the principles and strategies you will find within these pages.

In the first month, we focused on understanding the mindset shift required to embrace the 24-7 hustle. This involved researching successful individuals who have transitioned, analyzing their journeys, and distilling the key elements contributing to their success. We identified common themes such as setting clear goals, integrating hustle into daily life, and maintaining persistence despite obstacles. The insights gained during this month laid the foundation for the following chapters.

The second month was dedicated to practical strategies and tips for hustling 24-

7. We delved into time management techniques, productivity hacks, and the importance of continuous learning. We also explored ways to balance hustle with personal life, ensuring that the pursuit of success does not come at the expense of well-being. By the end of the second month, we had a comprehensive set of tools and techniques that anyone could implement to enhance their hustle.

The final month was spent refining the content, adding real-life examples, and ensuring that the book was informative but also engaging and entertaining. We wanted to create a book that you will not only learn from but also enjoy reading. Our goal was to strike the perfect balance between education and humor, making the journey of adopting a 24-7 hustle mindset as enlightening as possible.

Hustle, for the purpose of this book, means "assertive forceful, focused action to complete business goals successfully." This definition encapsulates the essence  of what it means to hustle 24-7. It is about being proactive, taking initiative, and continuously pushing towards your goals. This book has done that, providing a step-by-step guide to achieving your business goals through relentless hustle.

Why is this concept needed in today's world? The answer is simple: the traditional work model is outdated. In a world where technology and innovation are driving rapid change, the ability to adapt and seize opportunities is more important than ever. The 24-7 hustle mindset equips you with the tools to thrive in this dynamic environment, allowing you to break free from the constraints of a 9 to 5 job and create a lifestyle that aligns with your aspirations.

What will you gain from reading this book? You will learn how to shift your mindset, set clear and achievable goals, and integrate hustle into your daily life. You will discover practical tips for managing time, maximizing productivity, and staying motivated. You will also learn how to balance your hustle with your personal life, ensuring you maintain your well-being and enjoy a fulfilling lifestyle.

When is the best time to adopt a 24-7 hustle mindset? The answer is now. There is no time like the present to start taking control of your life and pursuing your dreams. Whether you are just starting out or looking to take your hustle to the next level, this book provides the guidance and inspiration you need to succeed.

Where can the principles of this book be applied? Anywhere. The 24-7 hustle mindset is versatile and can be used in various contexts, whether you are an entrepreneur, freelancer, or working in a corporate job. The principles and strategies discussed in this book are universal and can help you succeed in any field or industry.

How can you apply the concepts of this book in your day-to-day business? By taking assertive, focused action toward your goals. This means setting clear objectives, prioritizing your tasks, and continuously seeking ways to improve and innovate. It also involves building a solid network, managing your finances effectively, and learning from mistakes. Applying these principles will create a dynamic and successful business that thrives in today's competitive environment.

The world is full of opportunities, and the 24-hour hustle mindset allows you to seize them. It is about being proactive, staying motivated, and continuously pushing towards your goals. This book provides you with the tools and strategies to do just that. Each chapter is designed to guide you through the journey of adopting a 24-hour hustle mindset, providing practical tips and real-life examples to inspire and motivate you.

This book tells stories of individuals who have successfully transitioned from a 9 to 5 job to a 24-7 hustle lifestyle. These stories testify to the power of relentless hustle and the long-term rewards it can bring. Learning from their experiences will give you valuable insights and inspiration for your journey.

In addition to practical tips and real-life examples, this book also emphasizes the importance of maintaining balance and well-being. Hustling 24-7 does not mean sacrificing your health or personal life. Instead, it is about creating a harmonious balance that allows you to thrive personally and professionally. This book provides strategies for achieving this balance, ensuring you enjoy a fulfilling and sustainable lifestyle.

The conclusion of this book reflects on the journey and highlights the long-term rewards of the 24-7 hustle mindset. By embracing this lifestyle, you will unlock your potential, achieve your goals, and enjoy greater fulfillment. The journey may be challenging, but the rewards are worth the effort. This book is your guide, providing you with the knowledge and tools to thrive as a 24-7 hustler.

We hope that you will find this book both informative and entertaining. We aim to inspire and motivate you to embrace the 24-7 hustle mindset and relentlessly pursue your dreams. Remember, the journey of a thousand miles begins with a single step. Take that step today and start your hustle journey. The world is waiting for you.

In conclusion, "How to Hustle Twenty 47, Rather Than Slave 9 to 5: The Hustlers Pamphlet" is more than just a book; it is a manual for transforming your life. Over the following chapters, you will discover the secrets to breaking free from the traditional work routine and embracing a dynamic, goal-oriented lifestyle. Adopting the 24-7 hustle mindset will unlock your potential, achieve your goals, and enjoy greater fulfillment. We invite you to join us on this journey and embrace the power of relentless hustle. The world is waiting for you.

Chapter 1: Introduction – Breaking Free from the 9 to 5 Mindset

It was a cold Monday morning, and Jane's alarm buzzed incessantly, pulling her from a dream of sandy beaches and endless horizons. She groaned, knowing it was time to face another day in her  cubicle. But this day was different; it marked the beginning of her journey from the 9 to 5 grind to the exhilarating life of a 24-7 hustler. Jane's story is not unique — many are trapped in the routine cycle, craving freedom, and fulfillment. This book guides your GUI to being free, like Jane, and embracing the 24-7 hustle mindset that can transform your life.

The 24-7 hustle mindset is about a continuous, dynamic approach to achieving goals. Unlike the traditional 9 to 5 job that confines your potential within fixed hours, hustling 24-7 allows flexibility, creativity, and endless opportunities. It is not about working nonstop but optimizing your time and efforts towards meaningful pursuits. Adopting this mindset will enable a world where work and passion coexist harmoniously, leading to personal and professional growth.

Traditional 9 to 5 jobs come with their own set of limitations. The rigid structure often stifles creativity and limits growth. You are exchanging time for money, with little room for personal development. The 24-7 hustle, on the other hand, breaks these chains. It allows you to define your hours, work on exciting projects, and continually evolve. The hustle is about making every moment count and leveraging every opportunity to its fullest potential.

This book will guide you through adopting a 24-7 hustle mindset. Each chapter is designed to provide you with the knowledge and tools necessary to transition from a traditional job to a more fulfilling entrepreneurial lifestyle. We will cover everything from mindset shifts, practical tips for hustling, overcoming and obstacles, to balancing your personal life with your hustle. Whether you are looking to start a side gig, launch a full-blown business, or want to use your time better, this book is for you.

Our journey begins with understanding the mindset shift required to embrace the 24-7 hustle. We will delve into how to integrate hustle into your daily life, set clear and achievable goals, and learn from those who have successfully made the switch. You will discover hustling is not about burning out but working smarter and aligning your efforts with your passions.

In subsequent chapters, we will explore practical strategies to manage your time effectively, maximize productivity, and stay updated with industry trends. We will draw insights from successful entrepreneurs who have mastered the art of the hustle, providing you with actionable tips to implement in your own life. This is about creating a sustainable, high-energy approach to work that keeps you motivated and moving forward.

Transitioning from a 9-to-5 job to an entrepreneurial lifestyle can be daunting. But with the proper preparation and mindset, it is entirely achievable. We will guide you through assessing your readiness, planning your transition, and building a financial safety net. Real-life case studies will show how others have successfully navigated this journey, providing inspiration and practical advice.

Persistence is vital in the 24-7 hustle lifestyle. You will face obstacles, but this book will equip you with strategies to overcome them and maintain your momentum. We will discuss the importance of mindfulness and mental health, ensuring you stay resilient and focused on your goals. By learning from the experiences of well-known figures who have overcome significant challenges, you will be better prepared to tackle your own.

Networking is a crucial aspect of hustling. Building valuable connections can accelerate your success and open doors to new opportunities. We will cover effective networking strategies, leveraging social media, and maintaining relationships that support your hustle. Through examples of entrepreneurs who have thrived through networking, you will gain insights on how to build your own network.

Fiscal management is another critical component of the hustle. We will discuss budgeting, saving, and investing in your goals. Diversifying your income streams ensures economic stability and growth. Drawing from the experiences of successful hustlers, you will learn how to manage your finances wisely and invest in your future.

Embracing failure and learning from mistakes is part of the hustling journey. This book will help you reframe failure as a learning opportunity and develop resilience. You will grow more robust and capable by analyzing and learning from your mistakes. We will share stories of individuals who have turned their failures into steppingstones for success, providing valuable lessons for your journey.

Balancing hustle with personal life is essential for long-term success. We will explore strategies for maintaining work-life harmony, prioritizing well-being, and setting boundaries to prevent burnout. Through examples of individuals who have balanced demanding hustles with fulfilling personal lives, you will learn how to create a sustainable lifestyle that supports ambitions and personal happiness.

The conclusion will reflect on the long-term rewards of the 24-7 hustle mindset. We will recap critical lessons and strategies, highlighting the benefits of relentless hustle. An inspiring call to action will encourage you to embrace this lifestyle and passionately pursue your dreams. A memorable ending will leave a lasting impact, motivating you to start your hustle journey today.

Chapter 2: Adopting a 24-7 Hustle Mindset

The first step in adopting a 24-7 hustle mindset is shifting your perspective. Imagine viewing each day not as a series of hours to fill but as a canvas for your ambitions. 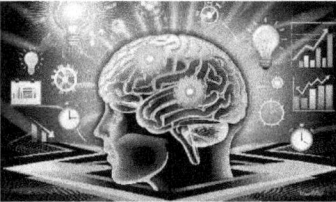 This mindset shift is crucial for breaking free from the traditional work routine. It is about seeing opportunities everywhere and realizing that your potential is not confined to office walls or a time clock. This chapter will guide you through this transformative process, helping you embrace a continuous, goal-oriented approach.

Incorporating hustle into your daily life requires deliberate effort and planning. It is not about working every waking moment but integrating your goals into your daily activities. This could mean dedicating specific hours to your side projects, using your commute time for brainstorming, or turning leisure activities into learning opportunities. By making hustle a natural part of your routine, you will ensure that you stay motivated and productive.

Setting clear goals is essential for a successful hustle. Your goals should be specific, measurable, achievable, relevant, and time-bound (SMART). This clarity will help you stay focused and track your progress. Whether your goal is to launch a business, learn a new skill, or increase your income, having a clear roadmap will make the journey smoother. We will provide tips and tools to help you set and achieve your goals effectively.

Consider the story of Alex, who transformed his passion for photography into a thriving business. Alex started by setting a goal to improve his skills and build a portfolio. He dedicated weekends to photo shoots and used evenings to edit and market his work online. Over time, his hustle paid off, and he was able to leave his 9-to-5 job to pursue photography full-time. Alex's journey is a testament to the power of clear goals and consistent effort.

Mindset shifts are not easy but necessary for adopting the 24-7 hustle. It is about embracing a new way of thinking and being open to change. This means letting go of limiting beliefs and replacing them with a growth mindset. Believing in your ability to learn, adapt, and succeed is fundamental. We will explore techniques to cultivate a positive and resilient mindset, setting you up for long-term success.

Daily integration of hustle involves balancing multiple aspects of your life. This requires effective time management and prioritization. It is about making conscious choices that align with your goals. For instance, instead of binge-watching TV shows, you might choose to spend that time working on a project or learning something new. You will make considerable progress without feeling overwhelmed by aligning your activities with your aspirations.

One key aspect of the 24-7 hustle is continuous learning. Staying updated with industry trends and acquiring new skills keeps you competitive and innovative. This could involve reading books, taking online courses, attending workshops, or networking with industry experts. Lifelong learning ensures you are always comfortable and ready to seize new opportunities. We will discuss many ways to integrate learning into your hustle routine.

Consider the example of Lisa, a marketer who transitioned to a freelance career. Lisa dedicated time each day to learning about digital marketing trends and tools. She attended webinars, read industry blogs, and experimented with new strategies. Her commitment to continuous learning improved her skills and expanded her network. Today, Lisa runs a successful marketing consultancy, all thanks to her dedication to lifelong learning.

Setting clear goals and integrating hustle into daily life are intertwined. Your goals should guide your daily actions, and your routine should support your goals. This constructive collaboration creates a powerful momentum that drives you towards success. We will provide practical tips to align your daily activities with long-term objectives, ensuring every effort counts.

The importance of setting boundaries cannot be overstated. While hustling 24-7, it is easy to blur the lines between work and personal life. However, maintaining a healthy balance is crucial for sustainability. This involves setting specific times for work, rest, and leisure. Establishing clear boundaries will burn out and keep your energy levels. We will share strategies to help you create a balanced and fulfilling lifestyle.

Networking plays a vital role in the 24-7 hustle. Building valuable connections can open doors to new opportunities and resources. Effective networking involves reaching out to like-minded individuals, joining professional groups, and leveraging social media platforms. Creating a solid network gives you access to support, advice, and collaboration opportunities that can accelerate your hustle. We will discuss tips and strategies for building and maintaining a robust network.

Another important aspect is investing in your hustle. This means dedicating resources—time, money, and effort—to your goals. Whether it is investing in education, tools, or marketing, making strategic investments will yield significant returns.

We will explore several ways to invest in your hustle, ensuring your efforts are efficient and effective.

Reframing failure is crucial for a successful hustle. Instead of seeing setbacks as roadblocks, view them as learning opportunities. Every mistake is a chance to grow and improve. You will build resilience and better prepare for future challenges by analyzing what went wrong and making necessary adjustments. We will share techniques to help you develop a positive attitude towards failure and learn from your mistakes.

Balancing hustle with personal life is essential for long-term success. This involves prioritizing self-care, maintaining personal relationships, and setting boundaries. Creating a healthy balance will ensure that your hustle is sustainable and fulfilling. We will provide tips and strategies to help you maintain this balance, ensuring you thrive personally and professionally.

Adopting a 24-7 hustle mindset is challenging but rewarding. By making mindset shifts, setting clear goals, integrating hustle into daily life, and balancing personal and professional aspects, you will set yourself up for long-term success. This chapter has laid the foundation for your journey, and the following chapters will delve deeper into each aspect, providing you with the knowledge and tools to thrive as a 24-7 hustler.

Chapter 3: Practical Tips for Hustling 24-7

Time management is a crucial skill for any hustler. Effective time management allows you to balance your work, personal life, and hustle without feeling overwhelmed. One strategy is to  break your day into blocks of focused work interspersed with short breaks. This technique, known as the Pomodoro Technique, can boost productivity and prevent burnout. By managing your time wisely, you will be able to accomplish more in less time.

Productivity hacks can significantly enhance your hustle. One such hack is the Two-Minute Rule: if a task takes less than two minutes to complete, do it immediately. This prevents small tasks from piling up and cluttering your to-do list. Another effective strategy is batching similar tasks together, which reduces the time spent switching between different activities. You will maintain high energy levels and achieve more by implementing these productivity hacks.

Continuous learning is vital for staying ahead in your hustle. This means keeping up with industry trends, learning new skills, and expanding your knowledge base. Online courses, webinars, and industry conferences are excellent resources for continuous learning. By investing time in education, you will stay competitive and innovative. We will discuss various platforms and resources that can support your lifelong learning journey.

Consider the example of Mark, a tech enthusiast who turned his passion into a successful side hustle. Mark dedicates time each day to learning about emerging technologies and trends. He followed industry blogs, participated in online forums, and attended tech meetups. His continuous learning paid off when he developed a groundbreaking app that gained massive popularity. Mark's story highlights the importance of staying updated and constantly improving your skills.

Effective time management involves prioritizing tasks based on their importance and urgency. The Eisenhower Matrix is a powerful tool that helps you categorize tasks into four quadrants: urgent and important, important but not urgent, urgent but not necessary, and neither urgent nor essential. By focusing on important and urgent tasks, you will ensure that your efforts align with your goals. We will provide tips on using this matrix to organize your tasks effectively.

Networking is a crucial aspect of hustling. Building valuable connections can open doors to new opportunities and collaborations. Attend industry events, join professional groups, and actively engage on social media. Networking is not just about what you can gain but also about what you can offer. You will create a strong and supportive network by building genuine relationships and providing value to others. We will share strategies to help you network effectively and make lasting connections.

Investing in your hustle means dedicating resources to your goals. This could involve investing in tools, education, or marketing. For instance, if you are starting an online business, investing in a professional website, and marketing campaigns can significantly boost your reach and credibility. Making strategic investments will enhance your productivity and help you achieve your goals faster. We will explore many ways to invest in your hustle wisely.

Reframing failure as a learning opportunity is crucial for a successful hustle. Every mistake is a chance to grow and improve. Analyze what went wrong, make necessary adjustments, and move forward. Developing resilience and a positive attitude towards failure will help you overcome challenges and stay motivated. We will discuss techniques to help you reframe failure and learn from your mistakes effectively.

Balancing hustle with personal life is essential for long-term success. This involves setting boundaries, prioritizing self-care, and maintaining personal relationships. Creating a healthy balance ensures that your hustle is sustainable and fulfilling. Set specific times for work, rest, and leisure to prevent burnout and maintain your energy levels. We will provide tips and strategies to help you effectively balance your hustle with your personal life.

Consider the story of Emma, who successfully balanced her demanding hustle with a fulfilling personal life. Emma set specific work hours and dedicated weekends to family and relaxation. She also prioritized self-care by incorporating regular exercise and mindfulness practices. Emma's approach allowed her to maintain high productivity without compromising her personal well-being. Her story illustrates the importance of balance in sustaining a successful hustle.

Effective time management also involves eliminating distractions. Identify and minimize activities that consume your time without adding value to your goals. This could mean limiting social media usage, setting boundaries with colleagues and friends, or creating a focused work environment. By reducing distractions, you will be able to concentrate better and achieve your goals more efficiently. We will share tips on identifying and eliminating distractions to enhance your productivity.

Networking can also involve seeking mentorship and guidance from experienced field professionals. Mentors can provide valuable insights, advice, and support as you navigate your hustle journey. Identify potential mentors, reach out to them, and build a relationship based on mutual respect and learning. By leveraging mentorship, you will gain a wealth of knowledge and accelerate your growth. We will discuss how to find and connect with mentors effectively.

Investing in your hustle also means investing in your personal development. This includes improving your skills, knowledge, and well-being. Consider enrolling in courses, attending workshops, or hiring a coach to support your growth. Personal development enhances your capabilities and ensures you are constantly evolving and ready to seize new opportunities. We will explore ways to invest in your personal development to support your hustle.

Reframing failure also involves celebrating your successes, no matter how small. Acknowledging and celebrating your achievements boosts your motivation and confidence. Recognizing your progress and rewarding yourself for your hard work is essential. This positive reinforcement will keep you motivated and focused on your goals. We will discuss ways to celebrate your successes and maintain a positive mindset.

Balancing hustle with personal life requires effective time management and prioritization. Create a schedule that allocates time for work, rest, and leisure. Stick to this schedule and adjust as needed. You will ensure you are productive and maintain a healthy balance by managing your time effectively. We will provide tips on creating and maintaining a balanced schedule to support your hustle and personal life.

In summary, practical tips for hustling 24-7 involve effective time management, productivity hacks, continuous learning, networking, investing in your hustle, reframing failure, and balancing your personal life. Implementing these strategies will enhance your productivity, help you stay motivated, and help you achieve your goals. The following chapters will delve deeper into each aspect, providing you with the knowledge and tools to thrive as a 24-hour hustler.

Chapter 4: Transitioning from a 9 to 5 Job to an Entrepreneurial Lifestyle

Transitioning from a 9-to-5 job to an entrepreneurial lifestyle is a significant step that requires careful planning and preparation.  The first step is assessing your readiness. Are you mentally and financially prepared to make the leap? Do you have an unclouded vision of your goals and a plan to achieve them? This chapter will guide you through the process of assessing your readiness and preparing for the transition.

Creating a strategic plan for your transition is crucial. This involves setting clear goals, outlining the steps to achieve them, and creating a timeline. Your plan should also include a financial strategy to ensure that you have a safety net in place. Planning your transition carefully will reduce the risks and increase your chances of success. We will provide tips and tools to help you create a comprehensive transition plan.

Building a financial safety net is essential before making the leap to entrepreneurship. This involves saving enough money to cover your living expenses for at least six months. Having a financial cushion will give you the security and peace of mind to focus on your hustle. We will discuss various strategies for building a safety net and managing your finances during the transition period.

Consider the story of Sarah, who successfully transitioned from a corporate job to entrepreneurship. Sarah spent a year preparing for her transition. She saved money, developed her business plan, and worked on her side hustle while still employed. When she finally made the leap, she had a financial safety net and a clear strategy. Today, Sarah runs a successful online business and enjoys the freedom and fulfillment of entrepreneurship.

Planning your transition also involves building a support network. Surround yourself with people who support your goals and can provide advice and encouragement. This could include mentors, fellow entrepreneurs, supportive friends, and family members. A solid support network will help you stay motivated and navigate the challenges of entrepreneurship. We will discuss ways to build and leverage your support network.

Marketing is a crucial aspect of entrepreneurship. Developing a marketing strategy to promote your business and reach your target audience is essential. This could involve creating a website, using social media, and running advertising campaigns. You will attract customers and build a strong brand presence by effectively marketing your business. We will provide tips and strategies to help you create and execute a successful marketing plan.

Transitioning to entrepreneurship also involves developing new skills. This could include skills in marketing, finance, and project management. Consider enrolling in courses, attending workshops, or seeking.

Mentorship to improve your skills. By continuously developing your skills, you will enhance your capabilities and increase your chances of success. We will explore several ways to build the skills needed for entrepreneurship.

Another important aspect of transitioning to entrepreneurship is managing your time effectively. As an entrepreneur, you will have more control over your schedule, so you must be disciplined and organized. Create a daily routine that balances work, rest, and leisure. Use time management tools and techniques to stay productive and focused. We will provide tips on managing your time effectively as an entrepreneur.

Building a brand is essential for entrepreneurial success. Your brand represents your business's identity and values. Develop a strong brand presence by creating a professional website, using consistent branding across all platforms, and engaging with your audience. By building a solid brand, you will attract customers and build trust. We will discuss strategies for creating and maintaining a solid brand.

Transitioning to entrepreneurship also involves taking care of your mental and physical health. Entrepreneurship can be demanding, so it is important to prioritize self-care and maintain a healthy lifestyle. This could involve regular exercise, mindfulness practices, and taking breaks to recharge. By taking care of your health, you will ensure that you have the energy and resilience to succeed. We will provide tips on maintaining your well-being as an entrepreneur.

Consider the story of John, who successfully transitioned from a 9-to-5 job to running his own business. John spent several months preparing for his transition, saving money, developing his business plan, and building a support network. When he finally made the leap, he had a clear strategy and the support he needed. Today, John runs a successful consulting firm and enjoys the freedom and fulfillment of entrepreneurship.

Networking is also crucial for entrepreneurial success. Building valuable connections can open doors to new opportunities and resources. Attend industry events, join professional groups, and actively engage on social media. Creating a solid network gives you access to support, advice, and collaboration opportunities. We will share strategies to help you network effectively and build lasting connections.

Marketing your business effectively is essential for attracting customers and building a solid brand presence. Develop a marketing strategy that includes online and offline channels. Use social media, email marketing, and advertising campaigns to reach your target audience. You will attract customers and build a strong brand presence by effectively marketing your business. We will provide tips and strategies to help you create and execute a successful marketing plan.

Managing your finances is crucial for entrepreneurial success. This involves budgeting, saving, and investing wisely. Create a financial plan that includes projected income, expenses, and savings goals. Monitor your finances regularly and adjust as needed. By managing your finances effectively, you will ensure your business is financially stable and growing. We will discuss various strategies for managing your finances as an entrepreneur.

Building a brand involves creating a solid and consistent identity for your business. This includes developing a professional website, using consistent branding across all platforms, and engaging with your audience. Your brand should reflect your business's values and mission. By building a solid brand, you will attract customers and build trust. We will explore strategies for creating and maintaining a solid brand.

In summary, transitioning from a 9 to 5 job to an entrepreneurial lifestyle involves assessing your readiness, creating a strategic plan, building a financial safety net, developing new skills, managing your time, building a brand, prioritizing your health, networking, marketing your business, and managing your finances. By following these steps and preparing carefully, you will increase your chances of success and enjoy the freedom and fulfillment of entrepreneurship.

Chapter 5: Overcoming Obstacles and Maintaining Persistence

Identifying challenges is the first step in overcoming obstacles. Familiar challenges hustlers face includes lack of time, financial  constraints, and self-doubt. Recognizing these challenges early on allows you to develop strategies to address them. This chapter will guide you through identifying and overcoming obstacles, ensuring you stay persistent and motivated despite setbacks.

Persistence is critical to overcoming obstacles and achieving success. This involves staying focused on your goals and working towards them, even when faced with difficulties. Develop a positive mindset and remind yourself of your goals and the reasons behind your hustle. By maintaining persistence, you will be better equipped to overcome challenges and stay on track. We will share techniques to help you stay persistent and motivated.

Mindfulness and mental health are crucial for maintaining persistence. Hustling 24-7 can be demanding, so it is essential to prioritize your mental well-being. Practice mindfulness techniques such as meditation and deep breathing to reduce stress and stay focused. Taking care of your mental health ensures you have the resilience and clarity to overcome obstacles. We will discuss various mindfulness practices to support your mental well-being.

Consider the story of Mike, who faced numerous obstacles while building his business. Mike encountered financial difficulties, self-doubt, and competition. However, he remained persistent and focused on his goals. He sought advice from mentors, practiced mindfulness, and continuously improved his skills. Today, Mike's business is thriving today, thanks to his persistence and resilience. Mike's story illustrates the importance of staying persistent and maintaining mental well-being.

Developing resilience is essential for overcoming obstacles. Resilience involves bouncing back from setbacks and continuing to pursue your goals. This requires a positive mindset, self-belief, and learning from mistakes. By developing resilience, you will be better prepared to handle challenges and stay motivated. We will provide tips and techniques to help you build resilience and overcome obstacles effectively.

Overcoming financial constraints involves strategic planning and resource management. This could mean budgeting, seeking alternative funding sources, or finding creative ways to reduce costs. By managing your finances wisely, you will be able to overcome financial challenges and invest in your hustle. We will discuss various strategies to help you manage your finances and overcome financial constraints.

Self-doubt is a common obstacle faced by hustlers. Overcoming self-doubt involves building self-confidence and trusting in your abilities. Surround yourself with supportive people, celebrate your achievements, and focus on your strengths. By building self-confidence, you will be better equipped to overcome self-doubt and stay motivated. We will share techniques to help you build self-confidence and overcome self-doubt.

Seeking support from mentors and peers can help you overcome obstacles. Mentors can provide valuable advice and guidance, while peers can offer support and encouragement. Build a support network of people who believe in your goals and can give constructive feedback. By seeking support, you will have access to valuable resources and motivation to overcome challenges. We will discuss ways to build and leverage your support network effectively.

Time management is crucial for overcoming obstacles related to lack of time. Effective time management allows you to balance your work, personal life, and hustle without feeling overwhelmed. Use time management tools and techniques to prioritize tasks and stay organized. By managing your time wisely, you will be able to overcome time-related challenges and remain productive. We will provide tips on managing your time effectively.

Consider the story of Lisa, who faced numerous obstacles while building her side hustle. Lisa struggled with time management, financial constraints, and self-doubt. However, she remained persistent and focused on her goals. She sought mentor advice, practiced mindfulness, and continuously improved her skills. Lisa's side hustle has become a successful business thanks to her persistence and resilience. Lisa's story illustrates the importance of staying persistent and overcoming obstacles.

Overcoming competition involves differentiating yourself and offering unique value. Identify your unique selling points and leverage them to petition. Focus on providing exceptional customer value and continuously improving your products or services. By differentiating yourself, you will be able to overcome competition and attract loyal customers. We will discuss strategies to help you differentiate yourself and overcome competition.

Maintaining a positive mindset is crucial for overcoming obstacles. A positive mindset involves focusing on opportunities rather than challenges and believing in your ability to succeed. Practice positive affirmations, surround yourself with positive people, and focus on your achievements. By maintaining a positive mindset, you will be better equipped to overcome obstacles and stay motivated. We will share techniques to help you maintain a positive mindset.

Overcoming obstacles also involves continuous learning and improvement. Stay updated with industry trends, seek feedback, and continuously improve your skills. Investing in your personal development will make you better prepared to handle challenges and stay competitive. We'll explore various ways to invest in your continuous learning and improvement.

Building resilience involves developing coping strategies for dealing with stress and setbacks. These strategies could include mindfulness practices, physical exercise, and seeking support from friends and family. By developing effective coping strategies, you can manage stress and stay focused on your goals. We will discuss various coping strategies to help you build resilience and overcome obstacles.

In summary, overcoming obstacles and keeping persistence involves finding challenges, developing resilience, managing finances, building self-confidence, seeking support, managing time, differentiating yourself, maintaining a positive mindset, and investing in continuous learning. By implementing these strategies, you will be better equipped to overcome obstacles and stay motivated on your hustle journey. The following chapters will delve deeper into each aspect, providing you with the knowledge and tools to thrive as a 24-7 hustler.

Chapter 6: Networking and Building Valuable Connections

Networking is a powerful tool for any hustler. Building valuable connections can open new  opportunities, resources, and collaborations. Effective networking involves reaching out to like-minded individuals, joining professional groups, and actively engaging on social media. This chapter will guide you through networking and building valuable connections to support your hustle.

The power of networking lies in its ability to create mutually beneficial relationships. Networking is not just about what you can gain but also about what you can offer. By building genuine relationships and providing value to others, you will create a strong and supportive network. We will share strategies to help you network effectively and make lasting connections.

Effective networking involves identifying and reaching out to potential connections. This could include attending industry events, joining professional groups, and participating in online forums. You will expand your network and build valuable connections by actively engaging with others in your field. We will

Discuss many ways to identify and reach out to potential connections.

Consider the story of Anna, who leveraged networking to grow her business. Anna attended industry conferences, joined professional groups, and actively engaged on social media. She built relationships with fellow entrepreneurs, industry experts, and potential clients. Through her networking efforts, Anna gained valuable insights, resources, and opportunities through her networking efforts that helped her business thrive. Anna's story highlights the power of networking and building valuable connections.

Leveraging social media is a powerful way to network and promote your hustle. Use platforms like LinkedIn, Twitter, and Instagram to connect with others in your field, share your expertise, and engage with your audience. A solid online presence will attract potential connections and build a supportive network. We will provide tips and strategies to help you effectively leverage social media for networking.

Building genuine relationships is crucial for successful networking. Focus on building trust and offering value to others. This could involve sharing your knowledge, offering support, or collaborating on projects. Building genuine relationships will create a solid and supportive network to help you achieve your goals. We will discuss ways to build authentic relationships and offer value to others.

Effective networking also involves following up and maintaining relationships. After meeting someone new, follow up with a personalized message or email. Stay in touch by sharing updates, offering support, and engaging with their content. Maintaining relationships will ensure that your connections remain solid and supportive. We will provide tips on following up and maintaining relationships effectively.

Consider the story of Tom, who used networking to accelerate his career. Tom attended industry events, joined professional groups, and actively engaged on social media. He built relationships with industry leaders, mentors, and peers. Through his networking efforts, Tom gained valuable advice, resources, and opportunities through his networking efforts that helped him achieve his career goals. Tom's story illustrates the importance of effective networking and maintaining relationships.

Seeking mentorship is a valuable aspect. Mentors can provide helpful insights, advice, and support as you navigate your hustle journey. Identify potential mentors, reach out to them, and build a relationship based on mutual respect and learning. By leveraging mentorship, you will gain a wealth of knowledge and accelerate your growth. We will discuss how to find and connect with mentors effectively.

Networking also involves giving back to your community. This could include volunteering, offering expertise, or supporting others. Giving back will build a positive reputation and create a strong and supportive network. We will explore ways to give back to your community and make valuable connections.

Building valuable connections also involves seeking feedback and learning from others. Be open to feedback and use it to improve your skills and knowledge. Engage in meaningful conversations and learn from the experiences of others. By seeking feedback and learning from others, you will enhance your capabilities and build a supportive network. We will provide tips on effectively seeking feedback and learning from others.

Effective networking requires active listening and communication skills. Listen to others, ask questions, and show genuine interest in their experiences and insights. By being an active listener and effective communicator, you will build more robust and meaningful connections. We will share techniques to help you improve your listening and communication skills for effective networking.

Leveraging social media for networking also involves sharing valuable content. Share your knowledge, insights, and experiences through posts, articles, and videos. By providing valuable content, you will attract potential connections and build a solid online presence. We will discuss strategies for creating and sharing helpful content on social media platforms.

Building valuable connections also involves collaborating with others. Look for opportunities to collaborate on projects, share resources, and support each other's goals. Collaboration can lead to new opportunities and strengthen your network. We will explore many ways to collaborate with others and build valuable connections.

Maintaining a positive and professional attitude is crucial for effective networking. Be respectful, courteous, and genuine in your interactions. Show appreciation for others' time and contributions. A positive and professional attitude will build a solid and supportive network. We will provide tips on maintaining a positive and professional attitude for effective networking.

In summary, networking and building valuable connections involve identifying potential connections, leveraging social media, building genuine relationships, following up, seeking mentorship, giving back, seeking feedback, active listening, sharing valuable content, collaborating, and maintaining a positive attitude. By implementing these strategies, you will build a solid and supportive network to help you achieve your goals. The following chapters will delve deeper into each aspect, providing you with the knowledge and tools to thrive as a 24-7 hustler.

Chapter 7: Financial Management for Hustlers

Budgeting and saving are essential skills for any hustler. Effective fiscal management ensures you have the resources to support your goals and maintain  economic stability. Create a budget that outlines your income, expenses, and savings goals. Monitor your finances regularly and adjust as needed. This chapter will guide you through budgeting and saving to support your hustle.

Investing in your hustle involves dedicating resources—time, money, and effort—to your goals. This could mean investing in education, tools, or marketing. For instance, if you are starting an online business, investing in a professional website, and marketing campaigns can significantly boost your reach and credibility. By making strategic investments, you will enhance your productivity and achieve your goals faster. We will explore many ways to invest in your hustle wisely.

Generating multiple income streams is crucial for financial stability and growth. Diversifying your income sources ensures that you are not reliant on an only source of income. This could involve starting a side hustle, investing in stocks, or creating passive income streams such as rental properties or online courses. You will increase your financial security and support your hustle by generating multiple income streams. We will discuss many ways to create multiple income streams.

Consider the story of David, who diversified his income sources to support his hustle. David started by creating an online store, then invested in stocks and real estate. He also created passive income streams by writing e-books and offering online courses. Through his efforts, David built a diversified income portfolio that provided financial stability and supported his hustle. David's story highlights the importance of generating multiple income streams.

Effective fiscal management also involves managing debt. If you have existing debt, create a plan to pay it off as quickly as possible. This could include consolidating debt, negotiating lower interest rates, or increasing your income to make larger payments. By managing your debt effectively, you will reduce financial stress and free up resources to invest in your hustle. We will provide tips and strategies to help you manage and pay off debt.

Investing in your personal development is another crucial aspect of monetary management. This includes improving your skills, knowledge, and well-being. Consider enrolling in courses, attending workshops, or hiring a coach to support your growth. Personal development enhances your capabilities and ensures you are constantly evolving and ready to seize new opportunities. We will explore ways to invest in your personal development to support your hustle.

Budgeting also involves tracking your expenses and identifying areas where you can cut costs. Use fiscal management tools and apps to monitor your spending and create a budget. Look for ways to reduce unnecessary expenses and save money. You will have more resources to invest in your hustle by managing your expenses effectively. We will provide tips on tracking expenses and cutting costs to support your financial goals.

Consider the story of Maria, who successfully managed her finances to support her hustle. Maria created a budget, tracked her expenses, and identified areas where she could cut costs. She also diversified her income sources by starting a side hustle and investing in stocks. Through her efforts, Maria built a solid financial foundation that supported her goals. Maria's story illustrates the importance of effective economic management and budgeting.

Investing in your hustle also involves making informed financial decisions. This means researching and evaluating potential investments, seeking advice from financial experts, and weighing the risks and benefits. Making informed financial decisions will enhance your productivity and help you achieve your goals faster. We will discuss several ways to make informed financial decisions to support your hustle.

Generating multiple income streams also involves identifying and leveraging opportunities. Look for opportunities to create passive income, such as investing in rental properties or creating digital products. Explore ways to monetize your skills and knowledge, such as offering consulting services or online courses. Identifying and leveraging opportunities will increase your financial security and support your hustle. We will provide tips and strategies to help you generate multiple income streams.

Effective fiscal management also involves planning. Create a financial plan that includes short-term and long-term goals, such as saving for retirement, building an emergency fund, or investing in your business. Monitor your progress regularly and adjust as needed. By planning for the future, you will ensure that you have the resources to support your goals and maintain financial stability. We will discuss various strategies for financial planning and goal setting.

Investing in your hustle also involves building a financial safety net. This includes saving enough to cover your living expenses for at least six months. Having a financial cushion will give you the security and peace of mind to focus on your hustle. We will discuss various strategies for building a financial safety net and managing your finances during challenging times.

Generating multiple income streams also involves leveraging your network. Build relationships with others in your field and look for opportunities to collaborate or support each other's goals. By leveraging your network, you will have access to valuable resources and opportunities that can help your hustle. We will explore ways to leverage your network to generate multiple income streams.

Effective economic management also involves setting financial goals and tracking your progress. Create specific, measurable, achievable, relevant, and time-bound (SMART) financial goals. Monitor your progress regularly and celebrate your achievements. By setting and tracking financial goals, you will stay motivated and focused on your financial objectives. We will provide tips and tools to help you set and track financial goals effectively.

In summary, fiscal management for hustlers involves budgeting, saving, investing in your hustle, generating multiple income streams, managing debt, investing in personal development, tracking expenses, making informed financial decisions, planning, and building.

A financial safety net, leveraging your network, and setting and tracking financial goals. Implementing these strategies will enhance your financial stability and support your hustle. The following chapters will delve deeper into each aspect, providing you with the knowledge and tools to thrive as a 24-7 hustler.

Chapter 8: Embracing Failure and Learning from Mistakes

Reframing failure as a learning opportunity is crucial for any hustler. Instead of seeing setbacks as roadblocks, view them as  chances to grow and improve. Every mistake is a valuable lesson that can help refine your approach and enhance your skills. This chapter will guide you through embracing failure and learning from your mistakes.

Analyzing mistakes is the first step in learning from them. When you encounter a setback, take the time to reflect on what went wrong and why. Identify the factors contributing to the mistake and consider what you could have done differently. By analyzing your mistakes, you will gain valuable insights that can help you avoid similar pitfalls in the future. We will provide techniques to help you effectively explore and learn from your mistakes.

Consider the story of Steve, who faced numerous failures while building his business. Steve's initial ventures were fraught with mistakes and setbacks. However, he took the time to analyze each failure, identify the lessons learned, and adjust his approach. Steve eventually built a successful business through his persistence and willingness to learn from his mistakes. Steve's story illustrates the importance of embracing failure and learning from mistakes.

Building resilience is essential for bouncing back from setbacks. Resilience involves developing a positive mindset, self-belief, and learning from mistakes. By building resilience, you will be better prepared to handle challenges and stay motivated. We will provide tips and techniques to help you build resilience and bounce back from setbacks effectively.

Embracing failure also involves celebrating your successes, no matter how small. Acknowledging and celebrating your achievements boosts your motivation and confidence. Recognizing your progress and rewarding yourself for your hard work is essential. This positive reinforcement will keep you motivated and focused on your goals. We will discuss ways to celebrate your successes and maintain a positive mindset.

Learning from others is another valuable aspect of embracing failure. Seek stories of well-known figures who have overcome significant obstacles and learned from their mistakes. By learning from the experiences of others, you will gain valuable insights and inspiration for your journey. We will share stories of successful individuals who turned failures into steppingstones for success.

Reframing failure also involves developing a growth mindset. A growth mindset is the belief that one can develop one's abilities and intelligence through effort, learning, and persistence. By adopting a growth mindset, one views challenges as opportunities for growth and embraces the process of learning and improvement. We will discuss techniques to help one cultivate a growth mindset and embrace failure as a learning opportunity.

Consider the story of Emily, who turned her failures into steppingstones for success. Emily faced numerous setbacks while launching her startup. However, she embraced each failure as a learning opportunity and continuously refined her approach. Her persistence and willingness to learn eventually led to her startup's success. Emily's story highlights the importance of developing a growth mindset and embracing failure as a learning opportunity.

Analyzing mistakes also involves seeking feedback from others. Constructive feedback can provide valuable insights and perspectives you may not have considered. Be open to feedback and use it to improve your approach and skills. You will gain valuable insights and accelerate your learning process by seeking feedback. We will provide tips on seeking and using feedback effectively.

Building resilience also involves developing coping strategies for dealing with stress and setbacks. These could include mindfulness practices, physical exercise, and seeking support from friends and family. By developing effective coping strategies, you can manage stress and stay focused on your goals. We will discuss various coping strategies to help you build resilience and overcome setbacks.

Embracing failure also involves maintaining a positive mindset. A positive mindset consists of focusing on opportunities rather than challenges and believing in your ability to succeed. Practice positive affirmations, surround yourself with positive people, and focus on your achievements. By maintaining a positive mindset, you will be better equipped to embrace failure and learn from your mistakes. We will share techniques to help you maintain a positive mindset.

Consider the story of John, who learned from his mistakes and achieved success. John faced numerous failures while building his business. However, he analyzed each mistake, sought feedback, and continuously improved his approach. John eventually built a successful business through his persistence and willingness to learn. John's story illustrates the importance of embracing failure and learning from mistakes.

Learning from mistakes also involves sharing your experiences with others. Sharing your mistakes and lessons learned will help others avoid similar pitfalls and contribute to their success. This also reinforces your own learning and growth. We will discuss ways to share your experiences and lessons learned with others effectively.

Building resilience involves staying focused on your long-term goals and maintaining your motivation. Remind yourself of your goals and the reasons behind your hustle. By staying focused and motivated, you will be better prepared to handle setbacks and continue pursuing your goals. We will provide tips on staying focused and motivated to support your resilience and growth.

Embracing failure also involves being patient and persistent. Success does not happen overnight, and setbacks are a natural part of the journey. Be patient with yourself and stay persistent in your efforts. By maintaining patience and persistence, you will be better equipped to overcome obstacles and achieve your goals. We will discuss techniques to help you maintain patience and perseverance.

In summary, embracing failure and learning from mistakes involves analyzing mistakes, building resilience, celebrating successes, learning from others, developing a growth mindset, seeking feedback, maintaining a positive attitude, sharing experiences, staying focused, and being patient and persistent. Implementing these strategies will turn failures into valuable learning opportunities and enhance your growth and success. The following chapters will delve deeper into each aspect, providing you with the knowledge and tools to thrive as a 24-hour hustler.

Chapter 9: Balancing Hustle with Personal Life

Work-life harmony is essential for long-term success. Balancing hustle with personal life involves setting boundaries, prioritizing 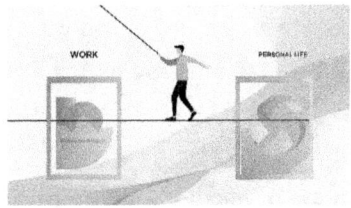 self-care, and maintaining personal relationships. This chapter will guide you through creating a healthy balance between your hustle and personal life, ensuring you thrive personally and professionally.

Maintaining work-life harmony requires effective time management and prioritization. Create a schedule that allocates time for work, rest, and leisure. Stick to this schedule and adjust as needed. You will ensure you are productive and maintain a healthy balance by managing your time effectively. We will provide tips on creating and maintaining a balanced schedule to support your hustle and personal life.

Prioritizing well-being is crucial for maintaining a healthy balance. This involves incorporating self-care practices into your routine, such as regular exercise, mindfulness, and adequate sleep. Taking care of your physical and mental health ensures you have the energy and resilience to succeed. We will discuss various self-care practices to support your well-being and balance your hustle with your personal life.

Consider the story of Rachel, who successfully balanced her demanding hustle with a fulfilling personal life. Rachel set specific work hours and dedicated weekends to family and relaxation. She also prioritized self-care by incorporating regular exercise and mindfulness practices. Rachel's approach allowed her to maintain high productivity without compromising her personal well-being. Her story illustrates the importance of balance in sustaining a successful hustle.

Setting boundaries is essential for preventing burnout and maintaining a healthy balance. This involves setting specific times for work, rest, and leisure and sticking to these boundaries. Communicate your boundaries with colleagues, friends, and family to ensure that they respect your time and space. Setting and enforcing boundaries will prevent burnout and maintain your energy levels. We will provide tips on setting and keeping boundaries effectively.

Balancing hustle with personal life also involves nurturing personal relationships. Be available for family and friends and engage in activities that strengthen your relationships. Building and maintaining solid personal connections provide emotional support and improve overall well-being. We will discuss ways to nurture personal relationships and effectively balance your hustle with your personal life.

Consider the story of James, who successfully balanced his hustle with his personal life. James created a schedule that allocated time for work, rest, and leisure time. He also was available for family and friends and engaged in activities that strengthened his relationships. By maintaining a healthy balance, James could stay productive and enjoy a fulfilling personal life. James's story highlights the importance of balancing hustle with personal life.

Maintaining work-life harmony also involves delegating tasks and seeking support. Do not hesitate to delegate tasks to others and seek support from your network. This allows you to focus on high-priority tasks and maintain a healthy balance. You will enhance your productivity and prevent burnout by delegating tasks and seeking support. We will provide tips on delegating tasks and seeking support effectively.

Balancing hustle with personal life also involves being flexible and adaptable. Life is unpredictable, and you may need to adjust your schedule and priorities occasionally. Be open to change and adapt your approach as needed. Flexibility and adaptability make you better prepared to handle challenges and maintain a healthy balance. We will discuss flexible and versatile ways to balance your hustle with your personal life.

Prioritizing well-being also involves taking breaks and recharging. Regular breaks and downtime are essential for maintaining your energy and preventing burnout. Schedule regular breaks throughout your day and take time off to recharge. You will enhance your productivity and maintain a healthy balance by taking breaks and recharging. We will provide tips on taking breaks and recharging effectively.

Consider the story of Karen, who successfully balanced her hustle with her personal life. Karen set boundaries, prioritized self-care, and made time for family and friends. She also took regular breaks and recharged to maintain her energy and productivity. Through her efforts, Karen achieved a healthy balance that supported her goals and well-being. Karen's story illustrates the importance of taking breaks and recharging to balance hustle with personal life.

.

Maintaining work-life harmony also involves setting realistic expectations and goals. Be realistic about what you can achieve within a given time and avoid overcommitting yourself. Setting realistic expectations and goals will prevent burnout and maintain a healthy balance. We will provide tips on setting realistic expectations and goals to support your hustle and personal life.

Balancing hustle with personal life also involves creating a supportive environment. Surround yourself with people who support your goals and respect your boundaries. Create a work environment that minimizes distractions and supports your productivity. Creating a supportive environment will enhance your productivity and maintain a healthy balance. We will discuss ways to create a supportive environment for balancing your hustle and personal life.

Maintaining work-life harmony
also involves practicing gratitude
and mindfulness. Take time each
day to reflect on your achievements
 and express
gratitude for the
positive aspects
of your life.
Mindfulness can
help you stay focused and present,
reducing stress and enhancing your
well-being. We will provide tips on
practicing gratitude and
mindfulness to support your
balance and well-being.

Consider the story of Lisa, who successfully balanced her hustle with her personal life. Lisa practiced gratitude and mindfulness, set realistic expectations, and created a supportive environment. Through her efforts, Lisa achieved a healthy balance that supported her goals and well-being. Lisa's story highlights the importance of practicing gratitude and mindfulness to balance hustle with personal life.

In summary, balancing hustle with personal life involves maintaining work-life harmony, prioritizing well-being, setting boundaries, nurturing personal relationships, delegating tasks, being flexible and adaptable, taking breaks and recharging, setting realistic expectations and goals, creating a supportive environment, and practicing gratitude and mindfulness. Implementing these strategies will enhance productivity, prevent burnout, and enjoy a fulfilling personal and professional life. The following chapters will delve deeper into each aspect, providing you with the knowledge and tools to thrive as a 24-7 hustler.

Chapter 10: Conclusion – The Long-term Rewards of the 24-7 Hustle

Reflecting on the journey of adopting a 24-7 hustle mindset, the rewards are well worth the effort. This chapter will recap the key  lessons and strategies discussed in the book, highlighting the relentless hustle's long-term benefits and rewards. By embracing this lifestyle, you will unlock your potential and achieve your goals.

The 24-hour hustle mindset is about making the most of every moment and leveraging every opportunity. It is not about working nonstop but about working and aligning your efforts with your passions. By adopting this mindset, you will experience personal and professional growth, increased productivity, and a greater sense of fulfillment. We will reflect on the journey and the benefits of embracing the 24-hour hustle mindset.

Consider the story of Jane, who transformed her life by adopting a 24-7 hustle mindset. Jane started by shifting her perspective, setting clear goals, and integrating hustle  into her daily life. She overcame obstacles, built valuable connections, and managed her finances effectively. Through her efforts, Jane achieved her goals and experienced the long-term rewards of relentless hustle. Jane's story illustrates the benefits of adopting a 24-7 hustle mindset.

Future success is another long-term reward of the 24-hour hustle. By continuously learning, improving your skills, and staying motivated, you will position yourself for long-term success. The hustle mindset ensures you are always constantly learning and ready to seize new opportunities. We will discuss the future success and growth of embracing the 24-hour hustle mindset.

The long-term benefits of the 24-7 hustle include financial stability, personal fulfillment, and professional growth. You will achieve economic security and support your ambitions by generating multiple income streams, managing your finances effectively, and investing in your goals. Personal fulfillment comes from aligning your efforts with your passions and achieving your goals. Professional growth is a result of continuous learning and improvement. We will highlight these long-term benefits and rewards.

An inspiring call to action will encourage you to embrace the hustle lifestyle and pursue your dreams relentlessly. The journey may be challenging, but the rewards are worth it. Adopting the 24-7 hustle mindset will unlock your potential and help you achieve your goals. We will provide an inspiring call to action to motivate you to start your hustle journey today.

Consider the story of Alex, who achieved long-term success by embracing the 24-7 hustle. Alex set clear goals, integrated hustle into his daily life, and continuously improved his skills. He built valuable connections, managed his finances effectively, and balanced  his hustle with his personal life. Alex achieved financial stability, personal fulfillment, and professional growth through his efforts. Alex's story illustrates the long-term rewards of the 2Adoptinge journey of adopting a 24-7 hustle mindset, which is challenging but rewarding. By making mindset shifts, setting clear goals, integrating hustle into daily life, and balancing personal and professional aspects, you will set yourself up for long-term success. This chapter has highlighted the benefits and rewards of the 24-7 hustle mindset, motivating you to relentlessly embrace this lifestyle and pursue your dreams.

The long-term rewards of the 24-hour hustle also include increased resilience and adaptability. By embracing failure, learning from mistakes, and staying persistent, you will develop these qualities, which are crucial for navigating challenges and achieving long-term success. We will discuss the benefits of increased resilience and adaptability that come with the 24-hour hustle mindset.

Reflecting on the journey also involves celebrating your achievements. Acknowledge and celebrate your successes, no matter how small. This positive reinforcement will boost your motivation and confidence. By honoring your accomplishments, you will stay motivated and focused on your goals. We will provide tips on celebrating your successes and maintaining a positive mindset.

The 24-hour hustle mindset also fosters a sense of community and support. By networking, building valuable connections, and seeking mentorship, you will create a strong and supportive network. This network provides helpful resources, advice, and encouragement, enhancing your journey and success. We will highlight the benefits of building a supportive community through the 24-hour hustle mindset.

Consider the story of Emily, who built a dedicated support network through her hustle. Emily leveraged networking sought mentorship and built genuine relationships. Her support network provided valuable resources and encouragement, helping her achieve her goals. Emily's story illustrates the importance of creating a supportive community through the 24-7 hustle mindset.

The long-term rewards of the 24-hour hustle also include personal growth and self-discovery. By continuously learning, taking on new challenges, and pushing your limits, you will experience these. This journey of growth and discovery enhances your capabilities and enriches your life. We will discuss the benefits of personal growth and self-discovery that come with the 24-hour hustle mindset.

In summary, the long-term rewards of the 24-hour hustle include personal and professional growth, financial stability,  resilience, adaptability, community support, and personal fulfillment. Adopting the 24-hour hustle mindset will unlock your potential and help you achieve your goals. This chapter has highlighted the benefits and rewards of relentless hustle, motivating you to embrace this lifestyle and pursue your dreams relentlessly.

Reflecting on the journey also involves looking forward to future opportunities and growth. The 24-7 hustle mindset ensures you are always constantly. You will achieve long-term success and growth by staying motivated, continuously learning, and embracing challenges. We will provide an inspiring call to action to encourage you to embrace the hustle mindset and pursue your dreams.

Consider the story of John, who achieved long-term success and growth through the 24-7 hustle. John continuously learned,  embraced challenges, and stayed motivated. He built valuable connections, managed his finances effectively, and balanced his hustle with his personal life. Through his efforts, John achieved long-term success and growth. John's story illustrates the benefits and rewards of the 24-7 hustle mindset.

In conclusion, adopting a 24-7 hustle mindset is challenging but rewarding. By making mindset  shifts, setting clear goals, integrating hustle into daily life, and balancing personal and professional aspects, you will set yourself up for long-term success. This chapter has highlighted the benefits and rewards of the 24-7 hustle mindset, motivating you to relentlessly embrace this lifestyle and pursue your dreams.

Check Out A Book Bundle From
Brian's Other Famous Titles
"How To Get Past The Gatekeepers and
Get To Your Goal In Life:
A Personal Guide to Being Persistent"

Bibliography

1. **Covey, Stephen R.** *The 7 Habits of Highly Effective People: Powerful Lessons in Personal Change*. Simon & Schuster, 1989.

2. **Hill, Napoleon.** *Think and Grow Rich*. The Ralston Society, 1937.

3. **Kiyosaki, Robert T.** *Rich Dad Poor Dad: What the Rich Teach Their Kids About Money That the Poor and Middle Class Do Not!*. Plata Publishing, 1997.

4. **Tracy, Brian.** *Goals!: How to Get Everything You Want Faster Than You Ever Thought Possible*. Berrett-Koehler Publishers, 2003.

5. **Sinek, Simon.** *Start with Why: How Great Leaders Inspire Everyone to Take Action*. Portfolio, 2009.

6. **Dweck, Carol S.** *Mindset: The New Psychology of Success*. Ballantine Books, 2006.

7. **Vaynerchuk, Gary.** *Crush It!: Why NOW Is the Time to Cash In on Your Passion*. HarperStudio, 2009.

8. **Cardone, Grant.** *The 10X Rule: The Only Difference Between Success and Failure*. Wiley, 2011.

9. **Ferriss, Timothy.** *The 4-Hour Workweek: Escape 9-5, Live Anywhere, and Join the New Rich*. Crown Publishing Group, 2007.

10. **Thiel, Peter.** *Zero to One: Notes on Startups, or How to Build the Future*. Crown Business, 2014.

11. **Collins, Jim.** *Good to Great: Why Some Companies Make the Leap... and Others Don't*. HarperBusiness, 2001.

12. **Schultz, Howard, and Joanne Gordon.** *Onward: How Starbucks Fought for Its Life without Losing Its Soul*. Rodale Books, 2011.

13. **Maxwell, John C.** *The 21 Irrefutable Laws of Leadership: Follow Them and People Will Follow You*. Thomas Nelson, 1998.

14. **Sincero, Jen.** *You Are a Badass at Making Money: Master the Mindset of Wealth*. Viking, 2017.

15. **Dalio, Ray.** *Principles: Life and Work*. Simon & Schuster, 2017.

NOTES